WAS IST LERNEN AN STATIONEN?

Beim Lernen an Stationen handelt es sich um eine Form selbstständigen Arbeitens, bei der

☐ unterschiedliche Lernvoraussetzungen,
☐ unterschiedliche Zugänge und Betrachtungsweisen,
☐ unterschiedliches Lern- und Arbeitstempo
☐ und häufig fächerübergreifendes Arbeiten

berücksichtigt werden.

Grundidee

Den Schülerinnen und Schülern werden Arbeitsstationen zur individuellen Bearbeitung angeboten, an welchen sie selbstständig, in beliebiger Abfolge und meist auch in frei gewählter Sozialform entsprechend ihren Möglichkeiten und Fähigkeiten arbeiten. Damit soll ihnen optimales Lernen und Üben ermöglicht werden.

Herkunft und Entwicklung

Die Idee des Lernens an Stationen, auch Lernzirkel genannt, kommt ursprünglich aus dem Sportbereich. Das „circuit training", von Morgan und Adamson 1952 in England entwickelt, stellt den Sportlern unterschiedliche Übungsstationen zur Verfügung, die sie der Reihe nach oder in freier Auswahl durchlaufen.

Eine Übertragung dieser Lernform auf Unterrichtsinhalte in verschiedenen Fächern wurde zunächst an der Schallenbergschule in Aidlingen/Baden-Württemberg, später am Seminar für schulpraktische Ausbildung in Sindelfingen und seit etwa 1980 an vielen Schulen aufgegriffen und stetig weiterentwickelt.

Der Herausgeber und die Autoren stellen die Ergebnisse ihrer eigenen praktischen Arbeit und Erfahrung in dieser Reihe vor und bieten ihre Materialien als Grundlage für den direkten Einsatz oder als Grundlage für eine Anpassung an eigene Bedürfnisse an.

Zielrichtungen

Das Lernen an Stationen kann unterschiedliche Ziele verfolgen:

☐ optimales Üben ermöglichen durch ein breites Angebot, das die verschiedenen Lerneingangskanäle, allgemeine Übungsgesetze, unterschiedliche Aufgabenarten, Schwierigkeiten und Hilfestellungen berücksichtigt,
☐ vertiefendes Bearbeiten eines Inhalts beziehungsweise eines Themengebietes, indem Schülerinnen und Schüler nach zuvor gestalteter Übersicht oder Einführung die Inhalte auf ihre Art, mit ihren Möglichkeiten und in ihrem individuellen Tempo auf unterschiedlichen Ebenen selbstständig bearbeiten,
☐ selbstständiges Erarbeiten von Themengebieten, indem die Schülerinnen und Schüler durch angemessene Arbeitsangebote Sachverhalte hinterfragen, erforschen, erfahren, gestalten usw.,
☐ Angebote aus Schulbüchern oder Medien unter ganz-

heitlicher Betrachtungsweise aufarbeiten, indem die Schülerinnen und Schüler Aufgabenstellungen zu Teilgebieten mit unterschiedlicher Betrachtungsweise und auf unterschiedlichen Ebenen fächerübergreifend bearbeiten.

Organisation

Die einzelnen Arbeitsaufträge geben den Schülerinnen und Schülern klare oder offene Aufgabenstellungen mit eindeutigen Anweisungen. Die Angebote werden im Klassenzimmer zur Verfügung gestellt, indem der Arbeitsauftrag durch Aushängen oder Auslegen bereitgestellt wird. Dazu bietet sich zum Schutz das Verpacken in Prospekthüllen an.

Als Ort zum Aushängen eignen sich alle Wand- und zum Teil auch die Fensterflächen. Pinn-Nadeln oder Nägel (Nagelleisten) erleichtern das Aufhängen und Abnehmen. Beim Auslegen der Arbeitsangebote bzw. -aufträge helfen Ablagekörbe, Ordnung zu halten.

Das Bereitstellen außerhalb der Schülerarbeitstische (also auf Fensterbänken, Nebentischen oder durch Aufhängen) erübrigt das tägliche Aufbauen und Wiederabräumen, stellt also eine große zeitliche und organisatorische Erleichterung dar. Falls im „Fachlehrerbetrieb" der ständige Abbau nötig ist, sind ineinander stapelbare Ablagekörbe, in denen die Aufträge verbleiben, sehr hilfreich. Die Kennzeichnung der einzelnen Stationen durch Ziffern, Buchstaben oder Symbole hilft den Schülerinnen und Schülern bei der Orientierung. Durch bewusste Verwendung dieser Ordnungsangebote kann die Struktur des Themengebietes oder eine andere Struktur (z. B. Arbeitsform o. Ä.) gleichzeitig verdeutlicht werden.

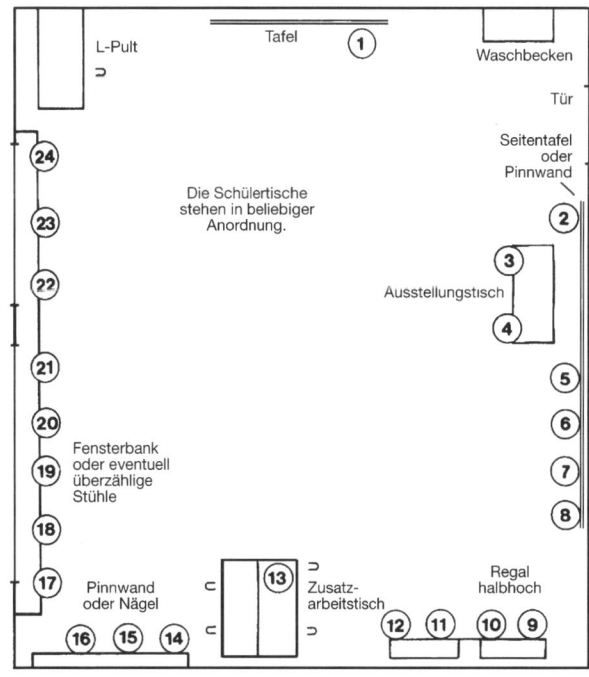

Eine Fortschrittsliste bzw. ein Laufzettel gibt Schülerinnen und Schülern wie den Lehrkräften jederzeit eine Rückmeldung über den derzeitigen Bearbeitungsstand und dient der Übersicht.

Auswahlangebote
Den Schülerinnen und Schülern ist sinnvollerweise ein Auswahlangebot zu ermöglichen; Minimalanforderungen können von der Lehrerin oder dem Lehrer definiert werden. Als Orientierungshilfe finden Sie dazu in den Hinweisen zu diesem Themenheft weitere Angaben.

Sonstige Tipps
Organisatorische Bedingungen und Festlegungen sind möglichst an der konkreten Situation und erst beim tatsächlichen Bedarf zu klären und zu regeln. Ist die Klassenstärke größer als die Anzahl der zur Verfügung stehenden Arbeitsstationen, können Sie die einzelnen Arbeitsaufträge mehrfach anfertigen. Weitere Hinweise zur Organisation, zu den Inhalten und zum Lernen an Stationen allgemein finden Sie im Einführungsband zu dieser Reihe, der unter dem Titel *Schülergerechtes Arbeiten in der Sekundarstufe I: Lernen an Stationen* beim Cornelsen Verlag Scriptor (ISBN 3-589-21117-2) erschienen ist.

Roland Bauer (Herausgeber)

ALLGEMEINE HINWEISE ZU DIESEM THEMENHEFT

Die vorliegenden Stationen machen die Schüler mit dem Thema *USA* vertraut. Auf der *Route 66* werden sie durch acht Länder der USA geführt und lernen Besonderheiten dieser Staaten kennen. Mit kurzen Texten zu Sachverhalten, die den altersspezifischen Interessen der Schüler entgegenkommen, erhalten sie landeskundliche Informationen und üben daran grammatische Aspekte sowie die Textproduktion.

Die vorliegenden Stationen sind zum einen in inhaltliche Bereiche untergliedert (*Route 66* und die acht Staaten, durch die sie führt), zum anderen in die Lernbereiche *Textarbeit*, *Vokabeln*, *Grammatik* und *Textproduktion*. Daraus ergibt sich folgende Matrix, die es erlaubt, auch einzelne Inhalts- oder Lernbereiche herauszugreifen:

		1 Text	2 Words	3 Grammar	4 Textproduction
A	Route 66	Get your kicks on Route 66	Route-words	The history of Route 66	Renting a car
B	Illinois	Chicago and the gangs	What is described?	Chicago's records	Giving directions in Chicago
C	Missouri	Missouri, St. Louis and the hamburger	How to make a hamburger	*Ing-form* or infinitive?	Ordering a meal
D	Kansas	Kansas and the Pony Express	Categories	In Dodge City	A letter to a friend
E	Oklahoma	Oklahoma and the Cherokee Indians	Connected words	Try to find the questions	Indian writing
F	Texas	Texas and the cowboys	WWW – Wild West Words	If you were a cowboy	A newspaper report
G	New Mexico	New Mexico and Billy the Kid	Jobs	Nations and nationalities	A picture story
H	Arizona	Arizona and the Grand Canyon	Sports and hobbies	Must – mustn't – may	Calling for help
I	California	California – the Golden State	Wordfinder	Prepositions	California Dreaming

Die Stationen berücksichtigen die verschiedenen Lerntypen ebenso wie unterschiedliche Methoden und Lerntechniken und lassen die unterschiedlichsten Sozialformen zu (Einzel-, Partner- und Gruppenarbeit).
Zur besseren Orientierung empfiehlt es sich, alle vier Stationen eines inhaltlichen Bereichs (A – Route 66, B – Illinois ...) jeweils auf gleichfarbiges Papier zu kopieren. Mit den Arbeitsblättern und den selbst erstellten Materialien kann auch ein USA-Buch zusammengestellt werden.

Die Lösungsblätter sollten auf jeden Fall getrennt von den Stationen aufbewahrt werden, z.B. an der Tafel oder einer Pinnwand.
Bei Stationen, für die alle Schüler ein eigenes Arbeitsblatt zum Ausfüllen benötigen, kann das Arbeitsblatt auch foliert und mit einem Folienstift beschriftet werden. Nach dem Löschen der Eintragungen kann es dann wiederbenutzt werden.

MATERIALLISTE UND ANMERKUNGEN

LAUFZETTEL VON: ....

Die folgenden Stationen habe ich schon geschafft:

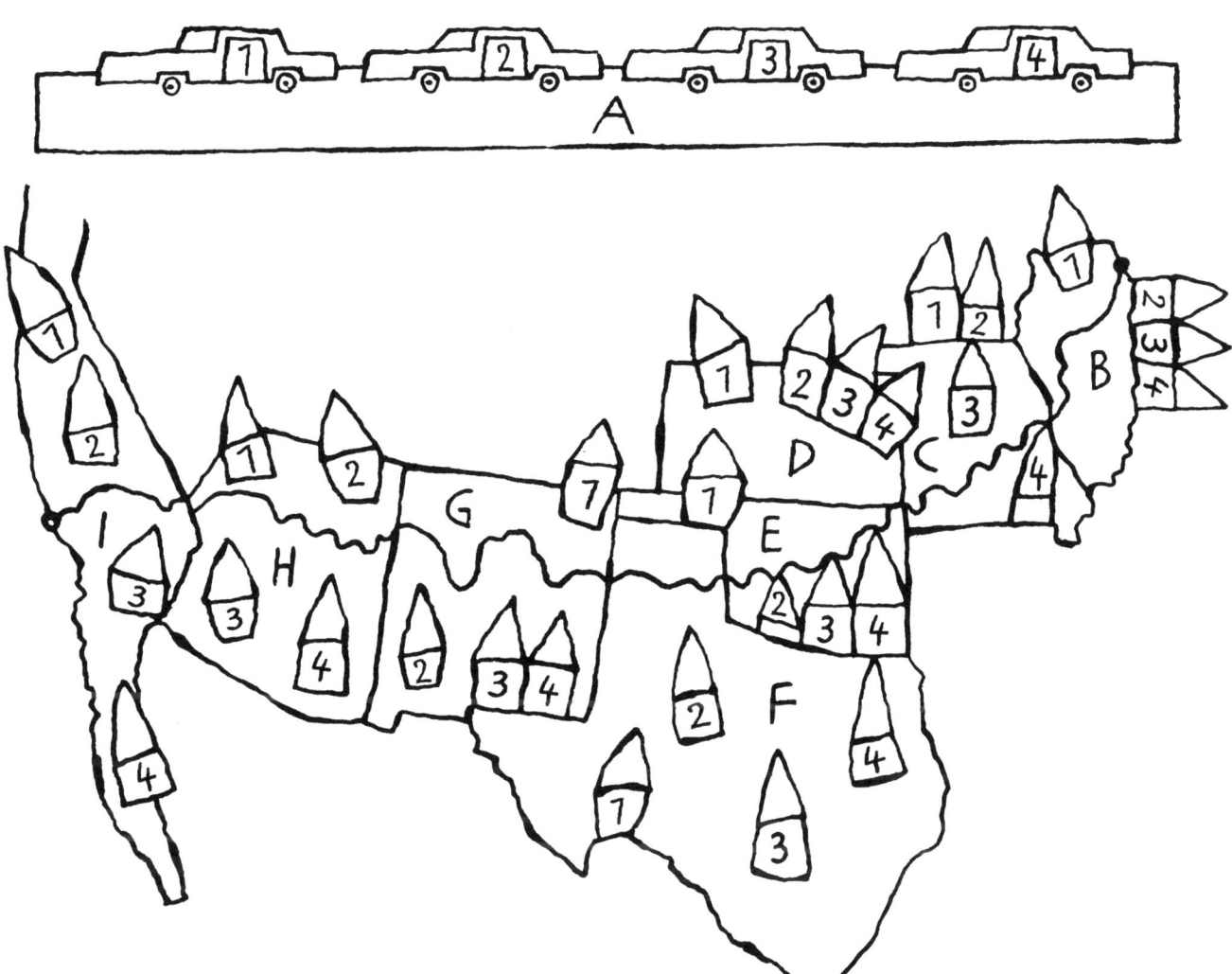

GET YOUR KICKS ON ROUTE 66

Go west! – From the beginning Americans went west. First on horseback and by wagon, later by train. They hoped to find land or gold and to start a new and better life in California.

Go west! – In 1903 the first car crossed the USA from east to west and in 1926 the most famous road was opened – Route 66. At the time the car was something exotic and extraordinary – and it was an adventure to drive a car. But if you think it was an amusing adventure or a dream to ride along Route 66 you are mistaken. It was hard to cross deserts and passes and to go through parts of America without a building or people for 2 400 miles. But you could go wherever you wanted by car – freedom. Driving a Chevy on a straight but stony road, watching the sunset and feeling the wind in your face – this is Route 66 today – the route that goes from east to west, from Chicago to Los Angeles. That's the route Americans call the Main Street of America and that the author John Steinbeck called Mother Road in his novel "Grapes of Wrath".

This route is special and it's synonymous with freedom. The freedom to cross the USA and to be on tour – free like a bird.

It's like a myth to be on Mother Road, that leads through eight states: Illinois, Missouri, Kansas, Oklahoma, Texas, New Mexico, Arizona and California.

So let's start on our way down Route 66.

GET YOUR KICKS ON ROUTE 66 – WORKSHEET

Have you heard about the legendary Route 66?

■ Read the text "Get your kicks on Route 66".

■ Look up any new words in your dictionary.
Write down the new words in your exercise book.

■ On the worksheet there are states you go through if you go west on Route 66. Colour them!

■ Take the map of the USA and mark the following cities on this worksheet: Chicago, St. Louis, Dodge City, Oklahoma City, Amarillo, Santa Fe, Flagstaff, Los Angeles.

Material: dictionary, map of the USA, colouring pencils

MAP OF THE USA

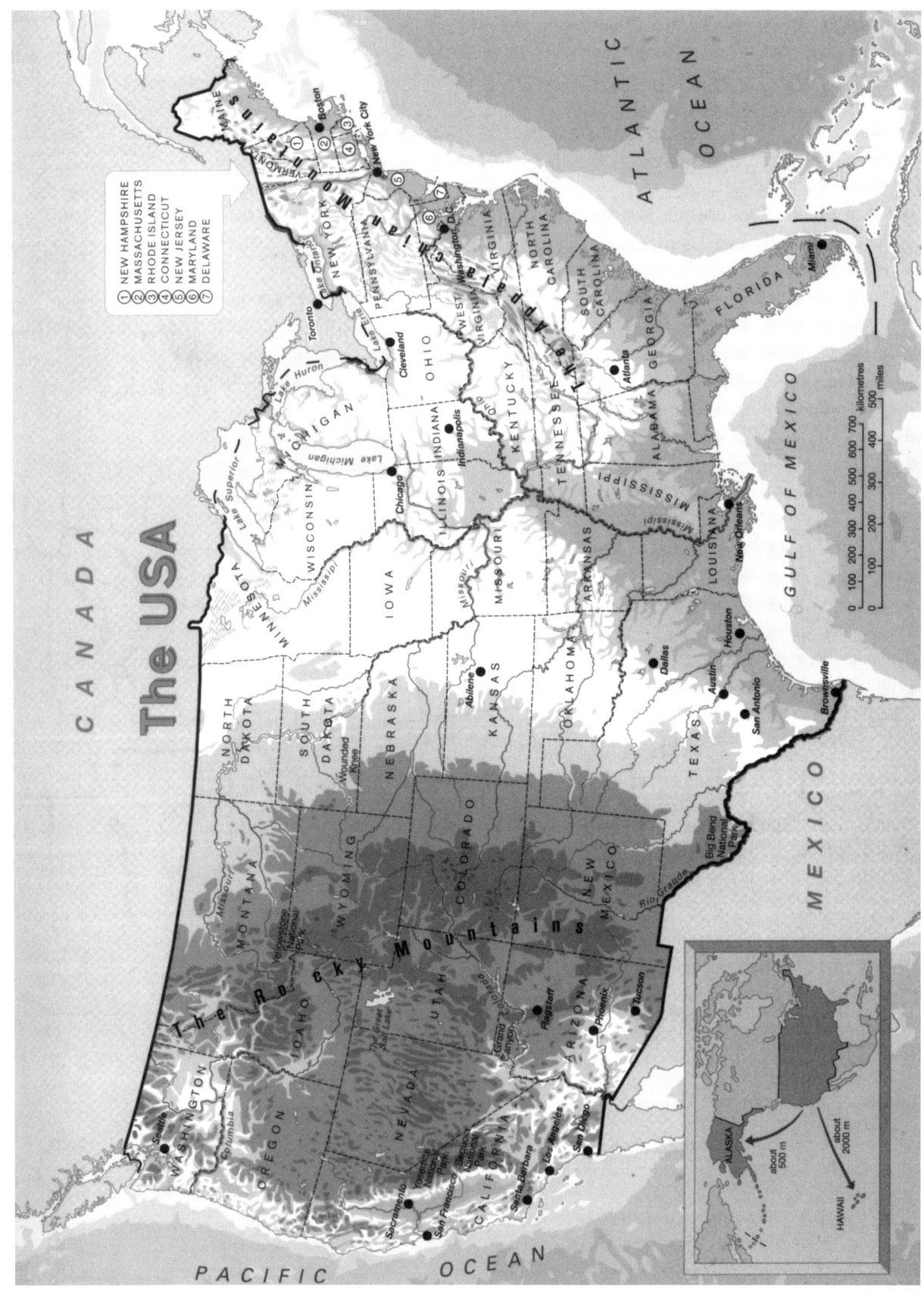

ROUTE-WORDS

Route 66 is associated with words like:
road, adventure, freedom, sundown, wind, Chevy, desert, go west

- Create a poster, showing a road, a Chevy ... Topic: Route 66

- Write the words that describe Route 66 on your poster.

- Give a definition of those words and write the definitions in your exercise book.

- Compare your definitions with the answer key.

Material: paper, pictures of Route 66, coulour pencils, scissors, glue, exercise book

THE HISTORY OF ROUTE 66

At the beginning of the 19th century there _____ simple trails all over the
USA. To get from east to west you _____ to follow those trails. Every state
_____ its own trails or roads, but they weren't connected.

In the 20th century eight states _____ to build a highway.

They _____ it US 66. In 1937 they _____ the street and
the first east-west-connection was finished.

In the thirties storms and bad harvests _____ poverty. People _____
of the Golden State California. So they _____ west. Some _____
California, some _____ and others _____ their fortune along the route.

After the 2nd World War a lot of people _____ peace.

They _____ to travel and _____ out to visit the National Parks
and other sights along the road.

But it _____ a small road and so President Eisenhower _____
Interstate 40 to be built.

People forgot Route 66.

But some years ago a _Route 66 Association_ was found that _____ it.

And so today you can still go along _Historic Route 66_.

■ Read the text.

■ Fill in the missing words (past tense!):
   be, have, have, start, call, open, cause, dream, go, reach, die,
   make, enjoy, want, go, be, order, revive.

■ Compare your solutions with the answer key.

RENTING A CAR

Imagine you are in Chicago at a car rental agency.

■ Try to make a conversation.
Sage, dass du ...
    ein Auto mieten möchtest,
    ein ... (Marke des Autos) möchtest,
    es für vier Wochen haben möchtest,
    es in Los Angeles abgeben willst.
Frage, ...
    wie teuer es ist,
    welche Versicherungskosten noch hinzukommen,
    ob es in den Staaten, durch die die Route 66 führt,
    Sonderbestimmungen gibt,
    ob du mit Creditkarte zahlen kannst.
Look up the words you need in a dictionary.

■ Write the sentences and questions on small cards.

■ Compare your sentences with the answer key.

■ Learn the sentences.

■ Act the dialogue with a partner.

Material: dictionary, small cards

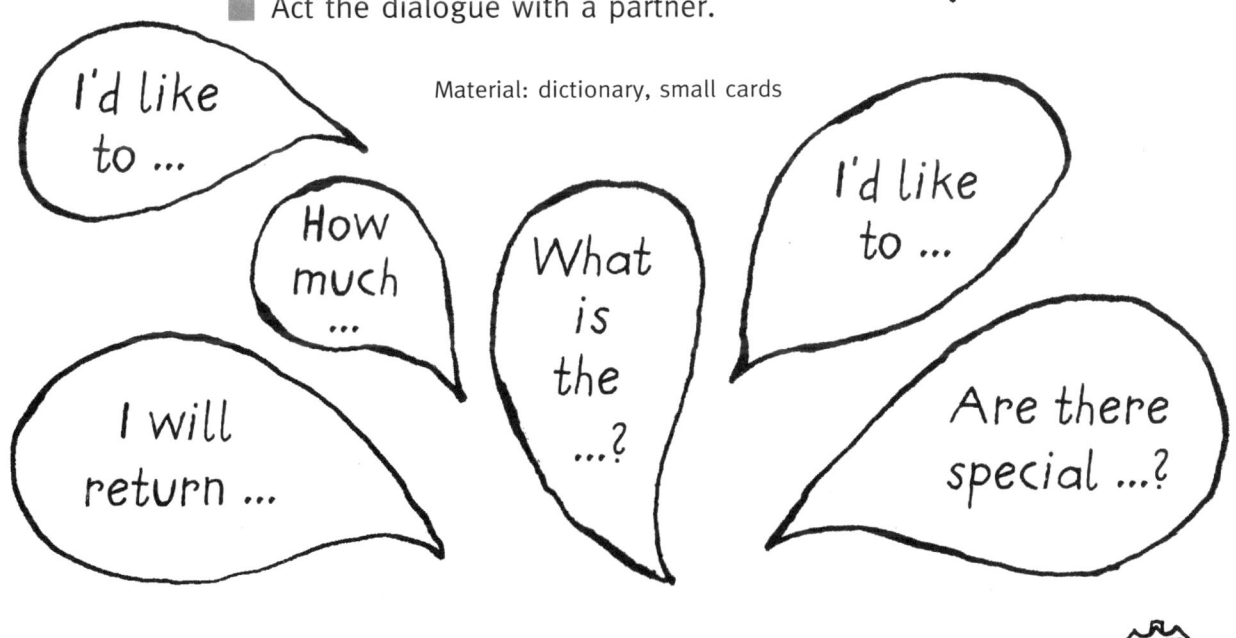

CHICAGO AND THE GANGS

The most famous city in Illinois is Chicago. It's the third biggest city in the USA. It lies on Lake Michigan, one of the five great lakes.

At the beginning of the 19th century Chicago was only a few small buildings. But a lot of people from many countries came here between 1880 and 1890. The price of land increased and so land-owners built towards the sky. In 1884 the Chicago School of Architecture with its famous architects Louis Sullivan and Frank Lloyd Wright built the world's first skyscraper with elevators in fireproofed material and metal. Today Chicago is famous for its skyscrapers. Sears Tower is one of the world's tallest buildings. It's 442 metres high and has 110 floors.

Chicago is also the city of Alphonse (Al) Capone, a famous gangster. In the 20th century there were a lot of gangs in Chicago: The Genna Brothers, O'Bannion, Bug, Alphonse ... They made money on the black market and by smuggling alcohol. The gangs started fighting when Al's enemy Bug robbed Al's alcohol transports. In revenge Al Capone killed seven of Bug's men in 1929.

So John Torrio, a leader of a gang, tried to explain that there would be enough money for all. So they made districts, paid money to governors and made contracts.

A lot of gangsters were killed but not Al Capone. He was caught by a tax officer and had to go to the prison on the island of Alcatraz in the San Francisco Bay, which became well-known because of its prisoner Al Capone.

- ▓ Read the text.

- ▓ Look up any new words and write them down in your exercise book.

- ▓ Try to find a title for each part.

- ▓ Compare your titles with the answer key.

- ▓ In those days a lot of people were killed in Chicago. There was a lot of crime and violence. What do you think, why isn't violence a way to solve problems? Discuss your opinion with a friend.

Material: dictionary, exercise book

WHAT IS DESCRIBED?

Try to connect the word and the right definition.

- On one side of a Triangle a sentence starts with a word that is defined on a second triangle. Put the triangles together so that you can read the whole sentence.

- If you put all the triangles together correctly they will make a bigger triangle again.

Material: Trimino

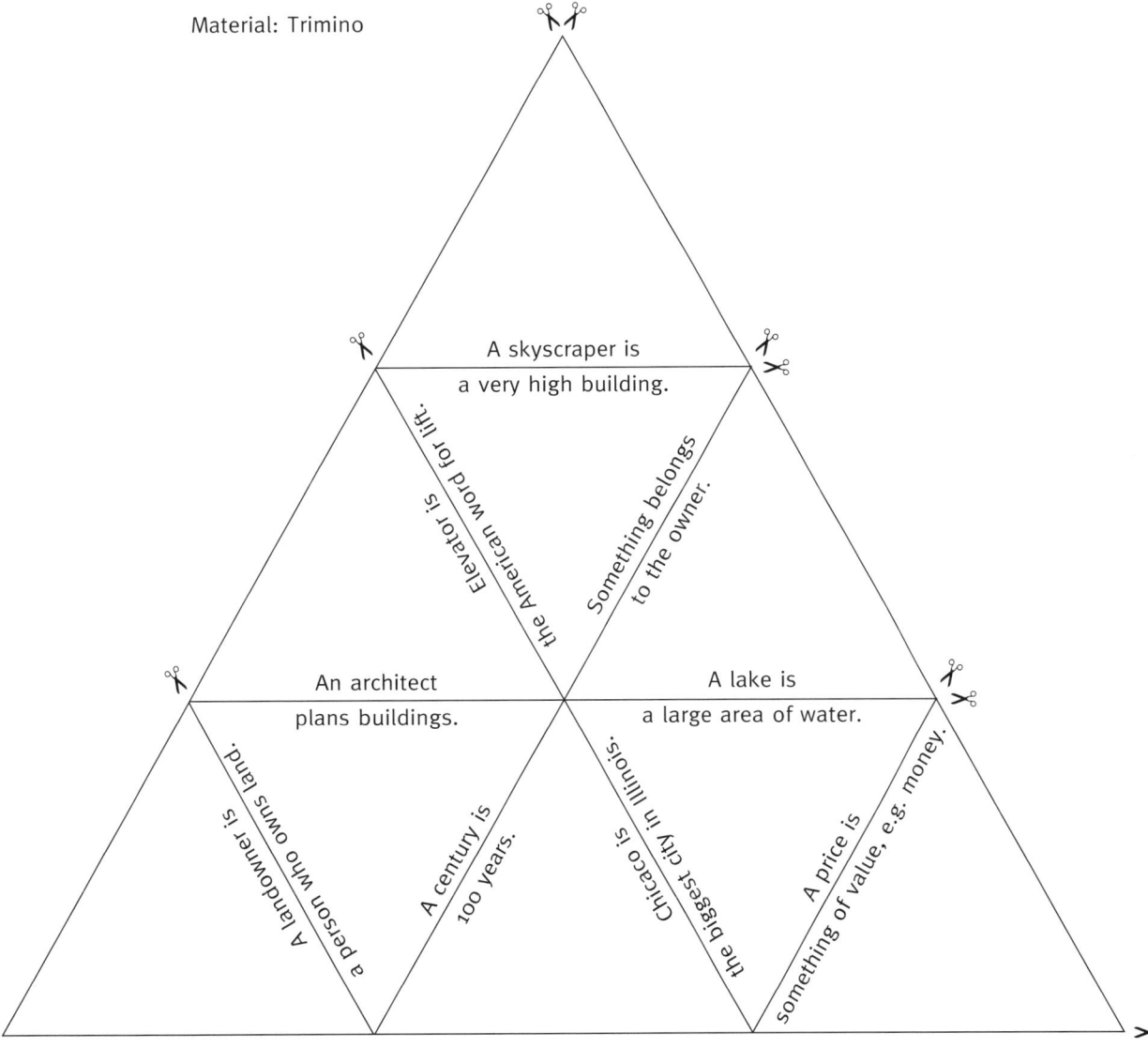

A skyscraper is a very high building.

Elevator is the American word for lift.

Something belongs to the owner.

An architect plans buildings.

A lake is a large area of water.

A landowner is a person who owns land.

A century is 100 years.

Chicago is the biggest city in Illinois.

A price is something of value, e.g. money.

CHICAGO'S RECORDS?

- Compare the things and persons mentioned on this worksheet.
  E. g.:   The Empire State Building is higher than ...
  The Sears Tower is smaller ...

Notice: Words with one syllable: -er, -est.
E. g.:   old – older – the oldest

Words with three and more syllables: more, the most.
E. g.:   frightening – more frightening – the most frightening

Words with two syllables follow one or other of the above rules.
E. g.:   boring – more boring – the most boring
clever – cleverer – the cleverest

- Write your answers in your exercise book.

- Compare your solutions with the answer key.

Material: exercise book, encyclopedia

(high) (small)	Sears Tower (442 m) (Chicago)	Empire State Building (443 m) (New York)
(dangerous) (famous)	Al Capone (gangster)	Billy the Kid (killer/hero)
(good) (interesting)	Chicago Bulls (basketball team)	Yankees (N.Y. basketball team)
(big) (small)	Chicago (2.7 Million inhabitants)	St. Louis (400 000 inhabitants)
(famous) (important)	Frank Lloyd Wright (architect)	Friedensreich Hundertwasser (artist)
(safe) (famous)	Alcatraz (prison-island in San Francisco Bay)	The Tower (prison in London)

GIVING DIRECTIONS IN CHICAGO

■ Work with a partner.

■ One person takes the town map of Chicaco and the other takes one of the instruction-cards.

■ Read the instructions on the card to your partner. Your partner has to follow your instruction. If he does so correctly he will end in front of the sight which is written on your card.

■ Change roles now. You take the map, your partner takes another instruction-card and reads it to you.

Material: map of Chicago, instruction-cards

INSTRUCTION-CARDS

You are in front of Sears Tower. Go along East Jackson Boulevard, turn left onto North State Street, go straight ahead, turn right onto West Washington Street, turn left onto North Michigan Avenue, the building is on the right side.
(Chicago Cultural Center)

You are in front of the Wrighley Building, go along South Michigan Avenue, turn right onto West Randolph Street, turn left onto South State Street, turn right onto West Washington Street, the building is on the left side.
(Brunswick Building Plaza)

You are in front of the Carson Pirie Scott & Store, turn left onto South State Street, turn right onto West Adams Street, turn left onto North La Salle Street, go straight ahead, the building is in front of you.
(Board of Trade)

TOWN MAP OF CHICAGO

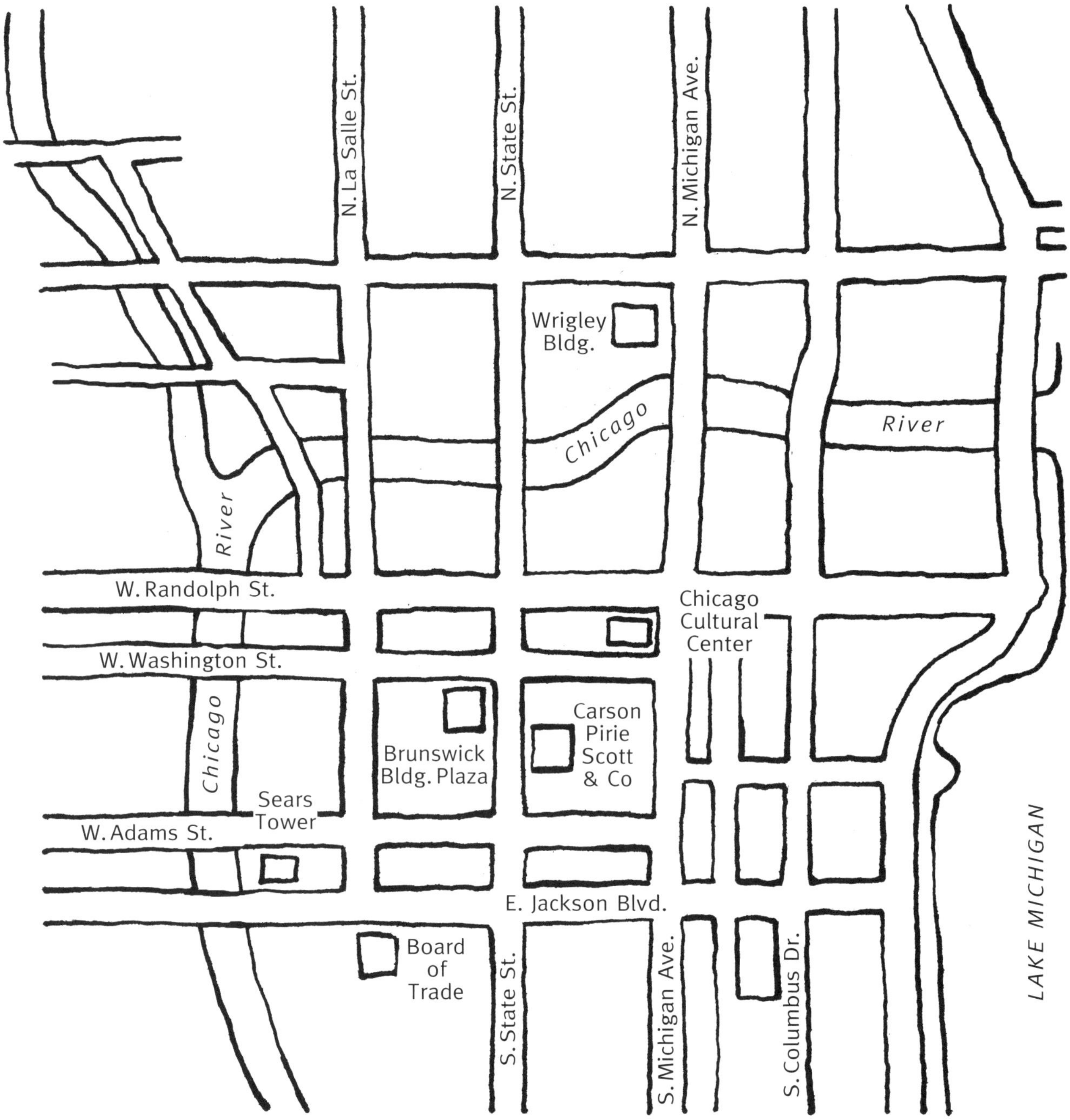

N. La Salle St.

N. State St.

N. Michigan Ave.

Wrigley Bldg.

Chicago

River

W. Randolph St.

Chicago Cultural Center

W. Washington St.

Chicago

Brunswick Bldg. Plaza

Carson Pirie Scott & Co

Sears Tower

W. Adams St.

E. Jackson Blvd.

River

Board of Trade

S. State St.

S. Michigan Ave.

S. Columbus Dr.

LAKE MICHIGAN

MISSOURI, ST. LOUIS AND THE HAMBURGER

Missouri is known by the two rivers Mississippi and Missouri, the great Lake of the Ozarks and the Ozark Mountains. St. Louis is a city in the north of Missouri where the two rivers Mississippi and Missouri meet. The new river is called Ol'Man River. From its beginning St. Louis was a trade center and got its name from the French King Louis the Saint. Up to the 19th century St. Louis was one of the most important cities west of New York. Treks going west started in St. Louis. The myth of adventure was something typical in St. Louis and so Charles Lindbergh called the plane he used to cross the Atlantic nonstop, "Spirit of St. Louis". The first Gemini Capsule that America launched into space was built in St. Louis.

But St. Louis is also famous for the hamburger. Originally the hamburger got its name from the German town Hamburg which was famous for its steak. German immigrants brought it to the USA. In 1904 the hamburger steaks were served on buns at the St. Louis World's Fair for the first time. Hamburgers on buns were easy to eat, really convenient and tasted good. So hamburgers on buns became the usual way of eating hamburgers.

- Read the text.
- Look up any new words in your dictionary.
- Write them in your exercise book.

Material: exercise book, dictionary

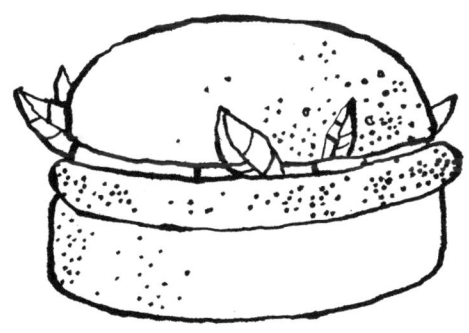

HOW TO MAKE A HAMBURGER

There are pictures showing ingredients for a hamburger. Can you explain in your own words how to make a hamburger?

■ Look up any new words in your dictionary.

■ Write them in your exercise book.

■ Find a partner.

■ Demonstrate to your partner how to make a hamburger.
Use the pictures to show the order of the ingredients.

Material: dictionary, exercise book, pictures of the ingredients

ING-FORM OR INFINITIVE?

Some words are followed by *ing-form*, some by infinitive.

> Note: These are some of the words that are followed by *ing-form*:

can't help	don't mind	enjoy	finish
give up	keep on	suggest	look forward to
succeed in	talk of	rely on	think of
be accustomed to	be fond of	be tired of	be used to
have difficulty in	be interested in	...	

- ◾ Find a partner.

- ◾ Make a sentence with each word and tell it your partner.

- ◾ Fill in the right forms on the worksheet.

ABOUT THE DIFFICULTY OF GETTING A HAMBURGER

Last year Michael decided _____ (go) to the USA.

He planned _____ (go along) Route 66 from Chicago to L.A.

He looked forward to _____ (drive) a Chevy.

After he managed _____ (get) his Chevy in Chicago, he wanted

_____ (get) a real American hamburger.

But he couldn't arrange _____ (get) into town.

He looked for a restaurant sign, but he didn't look at the traffic signs.

Michael got lost.

But he didn't give up _____ (look at) signs.

He drove around for hours.

Finally he succeeded in _____ (get) a hamburger in a smaller city –

it was St. Louis.

ORDERING A MEAL

You are in a restaurant in St. Louis.
You are very hungry and you want to eat something.

▧ Write the missing sentences on the worksheet.

▧ Act the conversation with a friend.

Waiter:	You:
Good evening. May I help you?	Frage, ob du die Speisekarte haben kannst.
Here you are. Would you like a cup of coffee?	Sage, dass du eine Tasse Kaffee mit Milch und Zucker möchtest.
Here is your coffee. Would you like to order something to eat?	Schau dir nun die Speisekarte an. Wähle eine Vorspeise, ein Hauptgericht, eine Nachspeise und ein Getränk. Bestätige und bestelle dein Essen.
Here is your drink and your starter. Enjoy your food.	

MENU

Starters

Mixed Garden Greens	$ 3.20
Tomato Salad	$ 2.50
Stir-fried Vegetables	$ 3.50
Ham and Melon	$ 4.30

Soups

Onion Soup	$ 3.10
Mulligatawny (Curry Soup)	$ 4.00
Vegetable Soup	$ 2.80
Soup of the day	$ 2.50

Entrees

Hamburger with Chips and Salad	$ 6.10
Chicken Breast with Mushroom Stuffing and French Fries	$ 7.50
Filet Mignon with Baked Potatoes and Salad	$ 11.10
Steak and Beans	$ 9.20
Cod Fish with Rice and Vegetables	$ 8.40

Dessert

Fruit	$ 2.00	Cheese	$ 3.50
French Pastries	$ 1.70	Ice-Cream	$ 3.00

KANSAS AND THE PONY EXPRESS

Kansas is often called the "Wheat State" or the "breadbasket of the USA", because it is covered with wheat fields. In summer you can see the wheat fields everywhere and it seems as if it is a huge sea of gold.

In the past it was very hard to grow wheat because there was little water in Kansas. Nowadays there are lakes and water reservoirs that help the farmers to water the fields.

One of the most famous cities in Kansas is Dodge City – perhaps you have heard the name in a western. Dodge City was a cowboy city and is a tourist attraction. In former times it was the largest cattle market in the world and had a courier station. Before the railways came to the west, the mail was carried by the couriers of the Pony Express. Their route took them through Kansas, too. The riders were younger than 18 and often orphans because it was hard and dangerous to ride through Indian land. They had to ride day and night. When they reached a station they jumped of the tired horse onto a fresh one and they were on their way again. On their way from east to west they needed 75 ponies and it took them ten to eleven days to get to California.

- Read the text.

- Look up any new words and write each one on a card – the English word on the front side, the German meaning on the back side.

- Learn the words.

- Find a partner. Ask your partner about the meaning of the words.

- Change roles.

- Create an advertisement-saying that you are looking for couriers. Try to include the following aspects. (Topic: Wanted. What are you looking for? Sex? Age? Responsibility! Payment! Duration of the job!)

Material: dictionary, cards, paper, colouring pencils

CATEGORIES

■ Which word doesn't belong with the others? Mark the wrong word in each line.

■ Compare your solutions with the answer key.

pony	sheep	cow	chicken
money	parcel	letter	postcard
wheat	potatoes	corn	rice
water	wet	dry	liquid
express	quick	fast	slow
station	horse	rider	saddle
river	lake	pool	basin
farm	road	stable	barn
railway	road	highway	river
January	season	summer	autumn

■ Find the generic term.

dog, cat, hamster = _pets_

summer, winter, spring, autumn = _____

wheat, oats, barley = _____

cow, ox, calf = _____

letter, parcel, postcard = _____

water, milk, lemonade, coffee = _____

house, stable, skyscraper = _____

boy, girl, man, woman = _____

fire, earth, air, water = _____

© Cornelsen Verlag Scriptor, Berlin • Lernen an Stationen • Themenheft »Englisch: USA – Route 66«

IN DODGE CITY

17 Pony Express Road
Dodge City
June 4th

Dear Peter,

At the moment I _____ (to sit) in the Saloon of Dodge City.

It _____ (to be) a Western Town which was rebuilt for tourists.

I _____ (to arrive) early in the morning.

In the morning the car park _____ (to be) empty and so I _____

(can) speak to the attendant. He _____ (to tell) me that a famous

actor would be there that morning. So I _____ (to decide) to sit in

front of the saloon and wait for the show. After I _____ (to wait)

for two hours and nothing _____ (to happen), I _____ (to go)

to the horse show. Suddenly I _____ (to hear) gunfires – I _____

(to run) back and saw Clint Eastwood. It _____ (to be) great.

Now I _____ (to relax) because the sun _____ (to be) hot and

I _____ (to be) thirsty.

I _____ (to drink) cold Coke at the moment.

Tomorrow I _____ (to go to) a Pony Express Station in the desert.

It _____ (to be) hot again tomorrow – I think I _____ (to take)

a big bottle of water with me.

Best wishes, Michael

■ Fill in the right tenses.

■ Compare your solutions with the answer key.

© Cornelsen Verlag Scriptor, Berlin • Lernen an Stationen • Themenheft »Englisch: USA – Route 66«

A LETTER TO A FRIEND

Imagine you are in a Western Town.

▩ Write a letter to a friend at home.
You should mention
- where you are
- where you are staying
- how you got to the Western Town
- who is with you
- what is special about the Western Town
- what happened
- what attractions you saw
- what you are going to do tomorrow

▩ Write it on a notepad first, your teacher will correct it then.

▩ Write it on notepaper after correction.

Material: notepad, notepaper

OKLAHOMA AND THE CHEROKEE INDIANS

At the beginning of the 19th century the Cherokee Indians lived in Tennessee and Georgia. It was good land and a lot of European settlers lived there, too. The Cherokee and the settlers lived in peace and didn't have any trouble.

But in 1830 gold was discovered in the mountains of the Cherokee. White settlers wanted to have the land and so the 16 500 Indians were told to go to Oklahoma by the government. The Cherokee didn't want to leave but the government sent soldiers.

All of them except a group of 4 000 Indians who went into the mountains, were put in camps and had to move west in a long wagon train. They had to travel 800 miles. It was a cold winter and a long distance.

Many Indians fell sick and nearly a quarter died because of cold, disease or hunger until they reached Oklahoma. All the others started a new life in Oklahoma but they couldn't forget the long and hard journey west. Therefore, they call it *The Trail of Tears*.

Nowadays there is a huge Indian reservation in the North of Oklahoma – the Osage Reservation, where you can find more than 30 tribes of Indians.

■ Read the text.

■ Look up any new words in a dictionary.

■ Take the map of the USA and try to find Oklahoma and the Osage Reservation.

■ What Indian tribes do you know? Tell your partner!

Material: dictionary, map of the USA

© Cornelsen Verlag Scriptor, Berlin • Lernen an Stationen • Themenheft »Englisch: USA – Route 66«

CONNECTED WORDS

It was a long and hard way west for the Cherokee Indians and a lot of them died because of cold, hunger or disease. So they called it the *Trail of Tears*.

■ Connect the words on the left with a word on the right.

■ Try to make sentences with these connected words and write them in your exercise book. Topic: Trail of Tears

■ Compare your solutions with the answer key.

Osage	soldiers
Cherokee	settlers
Trail	train
peaceful	journey
white	of Tears
wagon	reservation
move	Indians
hard	west
government	Cherokee

TRY TO FIND THE QUESTIONS

You've met a Cherokee and you want to know all about the Cherokee and the Trail of Tears.

■ Try to find the questions.

■ Compare your questions with the answer key.

1. _____

Yes, they lived in peace before gold was discovered there.

2. _____

The Cherokee live on the Osage reservation now.

3. _____

The white settlers wanted to have the land, therefore the Cherokee had to leave.

4. _____

4 000 Cherokee Indians went into the mountains.

5. _____

They had to travel 800 miles.

6. _____

Because of cold, disease or hunger.

7. _____

They started a new life in Oklahoma.

8. _____

They called it that way because it was a hard and long journey.

INDIAN WRITING

The Indians had a symbolic writing that was painted on buffalo skins.

◼ Try to read the Indian writing on the worksheet.
Follow the spiral drawing from the outside to the center.

◼ Write down the text in complete English sentences.

◼ Compare it with the answer key.

◼ Now write the text on a grey piece of paper that is torn like
a buffalo skin.

Material: worksheet, exercise book, a grey piece of paper, white pencil

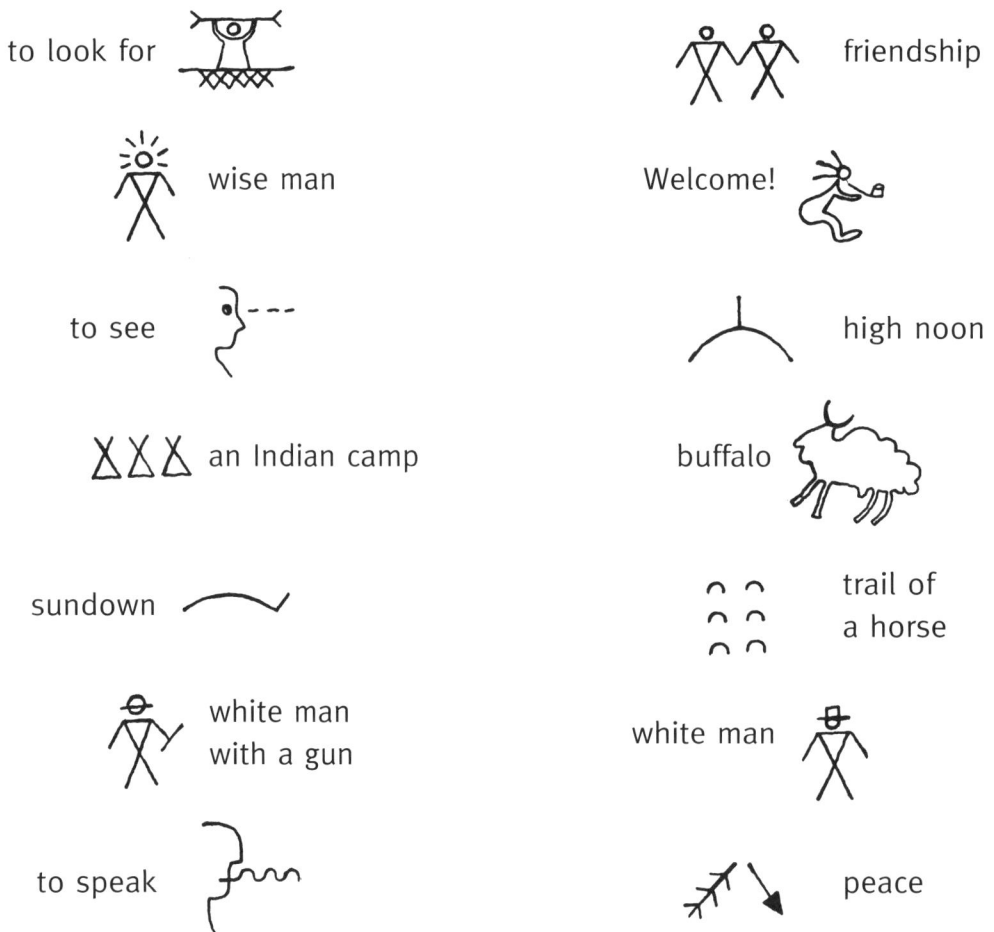

INDIAN WRITING – WORKSHEET

TEXAS AND THE COWBOYS

Texas is the largest state in America (except Alaska) and twice as big as Germany. You all know famous TV-series like Dallas or Texas Rangers, where Texas is shown with oil drills, farmland and cowboys.

In the past there were many cowboys, men who took care of cows and cattle on ranches. They had to look after them and bring them together in May and October. People in the north and the east of America wanted beef from the cattle and so the cowboys took the cattle to the next railway station. They had to ride with 2000 to 3000 cattle and travelled ten to twelve miles a day. So they had to work ten to fourteen hours a day, summer and winter. It took them many months and they had to stay with the cattle during that time. At the end the cowboys were happy to arrive at a place with a railway station where they got their money, a bath and new clothes. Today there are still cowboys on very big cattle ranches and they still ride horses when they are working. On Sundays they sometimes have rodeos to find who is the best cowboy. Those rodeos are exciting and dangerous. The cowboys have to pay $50 to start. Struck down by a bull while bare back riding, they often "kiss the dust".

■ Read the text.

■ Look up any new words in your dictionary.

Material: dictionary

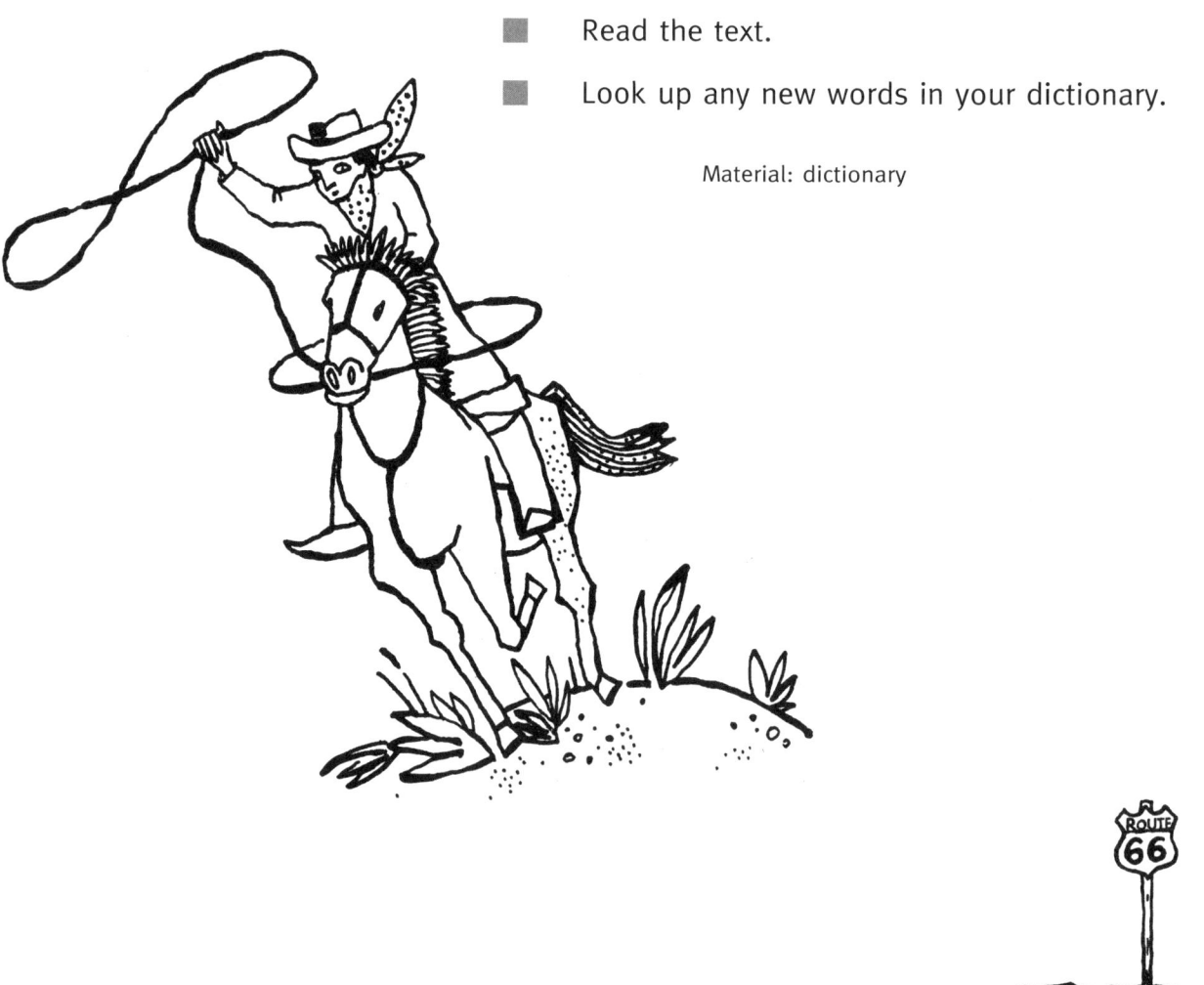

TEXAS AND THE COWBOYS – WORKSHEET

Texas is the _____ _____ in America. _____ _____,

_____ and _____ are typical for Texas.

In the past cowboys took 2 000 to 3 000 _____ to the next railway station.

It was _____ work because they had to work _____ to

_____ hours and to ride _____ to _____ miles a day.

Arriving at a _____ _____, the cowboys were happy. There they

got their _____, a _____ and new _____ .

Today there are still cowboys on _____ and they still _____

_____. On Sundays they sometimes have _____ to see who is

the _____ _____ .

■ Fill in the missing words without looking at the text "Texas and the cowboys".

■ Compare your text with the answer key.

WWW – WILD WEST WORDS

▨ Look at the picture.

▨ Try to find the words and write them in your exercise book.

▨ Compare your words with the answer key.

▨ Make a mindmap and collect words you connect with the topic:
Ranch

Material: dictionary, exercise book

IF YOU WERE A COWBOY

■ Imagine you are a cowboy. What would you do?

If I were a cowboy …
If I met an Indian …
If I lost cattle …
If I were robbed …
If I were thirsty …
If I arrived at a railway station …
If I had to sleep on the prairie …
If I got money …
If I had to cross a wild river …
If I saw a coyote at night …

Notice:
If-clause: verb in past tense   Main clause: verb in conditional tense
E.g.: If I were a cowboy   I would ride a black horse.

■ Write four dreams in the dream bubbles.

■ Compare your sentences with the answer key.

■ Cut out the dream bubbles and pin them on the pinboard
or glue them onto a poster.

Material: scissors, pinboard, glue, paper

A NEWSPAPER REPORT

You are at a rodeo in Texas.

- Try to write a report about the rodeo.

- The words mentioned will help you.

  Dallas – rodeo – Sunday – Southfork Farm – best cowboy – bare back riding –
  $ 50 – ten cowboys – fell down after three seconds – but John Willow – best – stayed on the back – one minute – winner got the prize money

- Perhaps you can write your article on the computer.
  Otherwise you can write it down into your exercise book.

- Show your report to your teacher, he/she will correct it.

  Material: computer or exercise book

© Cornelsen Verlag Scriptor, Berlin • Lernen an Stationen • Themenheft »Englisch: USA – Route 66«

NEW MEXICO AND BILLY THE KID

New Mexico is famous for its capital Santa Fe. In the past it was a market where Indians, Spaniards and Mexicans exchanged goods.

It is also famous for a person – Billy the Kid.

Nobody knows if he was a hero like Robin Hood or if he was a killer – but his biography is known. Billy's real name was Henry Mc Carthy. In 1861 his family moved to Kansas. But his father soon died. In 1873 his mother married again in Santa Fe, New Mexico. Billy was known as a very quiet and lovable kid.

He attended school and was really good at languages. He spoke Spanish, was polite and well-behaved. But he wasn't harmless. At the age of 14 Billy shot a blacksmith who offended his mother. Then he left home and travelled around.

After being a cowboy, a gambler, a gold digger and a fortune seeker in New Mexico, Texas, Arizona and Mexico, he got a job in Lincoln, New Mexico. There he shot the sheriff and the co-sheriff in a quarrel and was chased. In summer 1880 he was caught at Fort Summner in New Mexico and brought to prison.

They wanted to hang him but he escaped. After one year he returned to Fort Summner to visit a friend. But Sheriff Garett was waiting at Billy's friend that night and shot him when he entered the room.

▓ Read the text.

▓ Look up any new words in your dictionary.

▓ Create a Billy the Kid-Wanted-Poster. It should include: real name – his behavior – his knowledge – what happened to the blacksmith – where Billy travelled around – what happened in Lincoln

Material: dictionary, paper, colouring pencils

JOBS

Let's play a game like the German *Stadt-Land-Fluss*.

◼ Find two or three partners.

◼ Everyone creates a list like the following one:

points	job	tool	verb
	cowboy	computer	carry

◼ One person says "A" and continues saying the alphabet silently.

◼ A second person says "Stop!".

◼ Now you have to write down a job, tool …, starting with the letter mentioned.

◼ The one who has finished first says "Stop!".

◼ You will get the following points:
20 points if nobody has a word in this column.
10 points if no one has the same word in this column.

Material: paper, ruler, pencil

NATIONS AND NATIONALITIES

■ Fill in the missing nations or nationalities.

■ Look up the words you need in your dictionary.

■ Compare your solutions with the answer key.

the country	one person	the people
Mexico		
	an American	
		the Spanish
	a German	
Canada		
		the Portuguese
		the British
China		
	an Asian	
Puerto Rico		
		the Italians

A PICTURE STORY

Perhaps you know the western "High Noon".
Some movie scenes are shown in the pictures below.

■ Try to write the story. The pictures and words will help you.

■ Compare your story with the answer key.

Material: exercise book

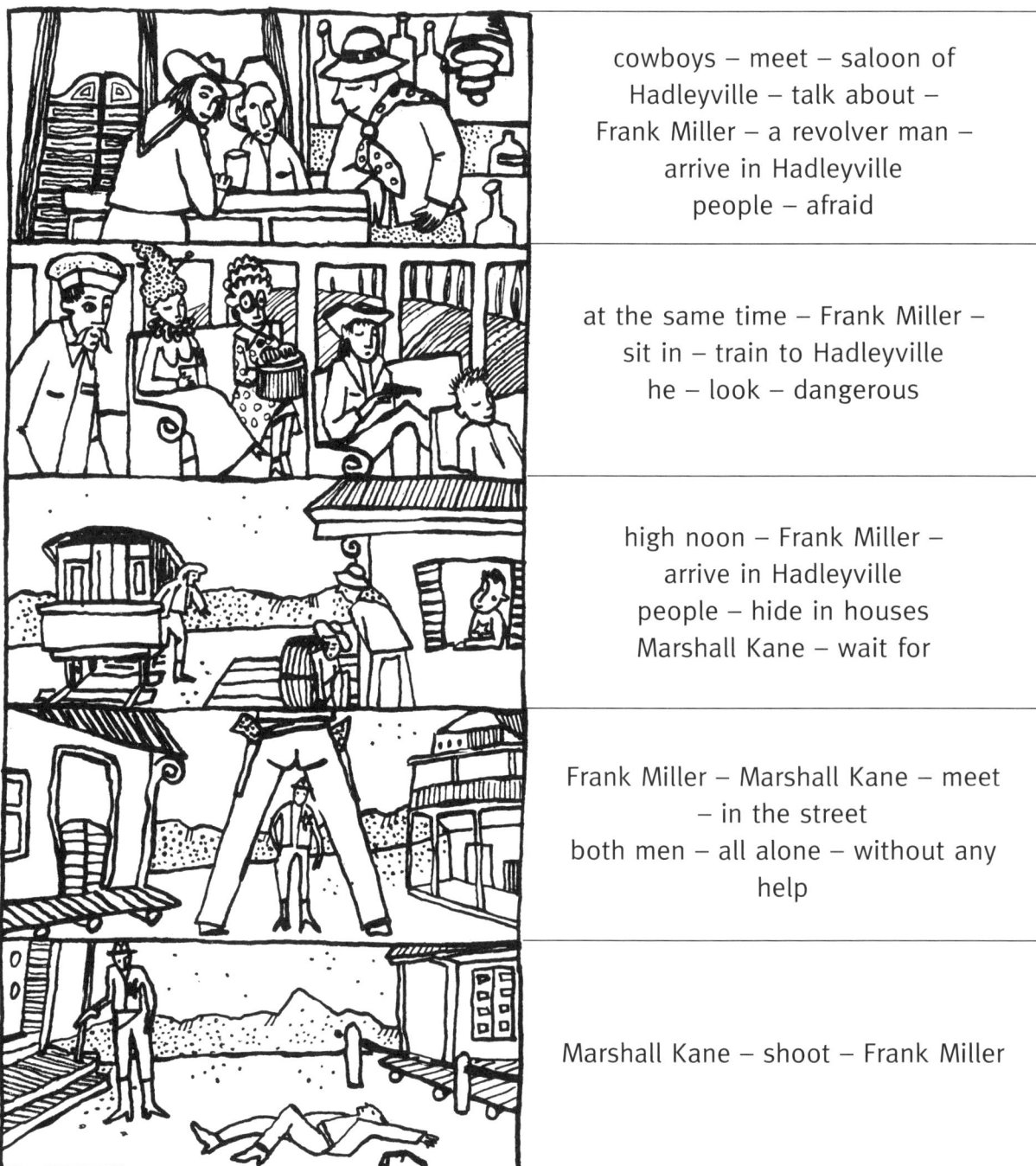

	cowboys – meet – saloon of Hadleyville – talk about – Frank Miller – a revolver man – arrive in Hadleyville people – afraid
	at the same time – Frank Miller – sit in – train to Hadleyville he – look – dangerous
	high noon – Frank Miller – arrive in Hadleyville people – hide in houses Marshall Kane – wait for
	Frank Miller – Marshall Kane – meet – in the street both men – all alone – without any help
	Marshall Kane – shoot – Frank Miller

ARIZONA AND THE GRAND CANYON

Arizona is famous for its Grand Canyon National Park. On the North and the South Rim of the canyon you can enjoy fantastic views.
There are trails to the Colorado River down at the bottom. The Grand Canyon is one mile deep. If you want to walk down to the bottom, you have to be prepared. You start your tour at the tourist centre at the Grand Canyon. Because it's very hot in the canyon people start early in the morning and take a lot of drinking water with them. It's a steep path with lots of bends. It only takes four hours to the bottom of the canyon. But the way back takes about eight hours. You walk downhill when you are fit but uphill when you are tired. So you should never try to get to the river and back in one day. You can sleep at the Phantom Ranch at the bottom of the Grand Canyon. Although there are signs telling the tourists not to do the tour in one day, every year rangers have to help more than 200 tourists to get back.
If someone can't walk any longer there is one essential rule for hiking in the Grand Canyon: Never leave a hiker alone in the canyon!

   ■ Read the text.

   ■ Look up any new words in a dictionary.
     Write down the words in your exercise book.

   ■ Answer the questions and you will have a summary of of the text.
     Write the answers in your exercise book.

   ■ Compare your sentences with the answer key.

What is fantastic?	... is fantastic.
Why is it difficult?	But it's ... because ...
Where can you start?	You can ...
Why do you have to take a lot of water with you?	You have to take ... because ...
How long does it take to go down and up?	It takes ...
What's the problem?	The problem is ...
What important rule is there?	There is one important ...
What do rangers often have to do?	Rangers ...

Material: dictionary, exercise book

© Cornelsen Verlag Scriptor, Berlin • Lernen an Stationen • Themenheft »Englisch: USA – Route 66«

SPORTS AND HOBBIES

■ Try to find as many words as possible connected with sports. The pictograms will help you.

■ Write down the words in your exercise book.

■ Compare your words with the answer key.

Material: dictionary

■ Try to find as many words as possible connected with other hobbies. You can look in the dictionary, too.

■ Write down the words in your exercise book.

MUST – MUSTN'T – MAY

There are park rules in every National Park.
So there are rules in the Grand Canyon, too.

■ Write down park rules using *must – mustn't – may*.
The words below will help you.
Help: *must* – müssen, *mustn't* – nicht dürfen, *may* – dürfen

hiking shoes	water	go alone
in one day	early in the morning	sandals
leave the trail	trained	leave a hiker
get a ranger sometimes	take photos	

■ Write these rules on coloured paper and create a poster as if it is a sign that is put up in the canyon.

■ Compare your rules with the answer key.

Material: coloured paper

© Cornelsen Verlag Scriptor, Berlin • Lernen an Stationen • Themenheft »Englisch: USA – Route 66«

CALLING FOR HELP

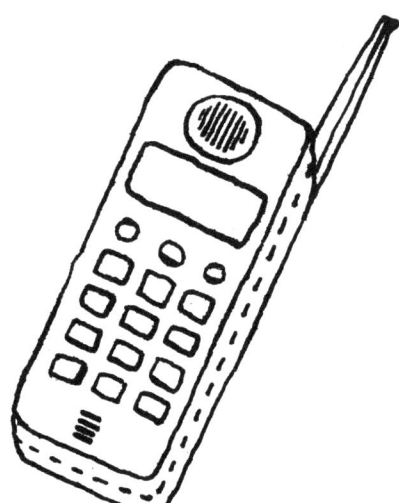

You are in the canyon with your friend, but she can't walk anymore. You started early in the morning, but you went down to the Colorado River and back again. One hour before Cedar Ridge, you've drunken all the water you had with you.

▪ Write down a cell-phone-call with a ranger.

▪ Compare your dialogue with the answer key.

You	Ranger
Hello, this is _____ speaking. I need help!	
	Hello! What's the matter?
	Are you alone?
	What happened?
	Where are you?
	Have you got enough water?
	Okay then, stay where you are. We will arrive as soon as possible. If there are any problems, call me again.
	Bye!

CALIFORNIA – THE GOLDEN STATE

California Dreaming – wind – sun and waves – this is California. California is called the Golden State because its modern development can be traced back to the discovery of gold in 1848. It's sunny all the year and so the people like to visit California or live there.

There are famous cities like San Francisco and Los Angeles. San Francisco is known for the Golden Gate Bridge, cablecars and Chinatown.

Los Angeles is famous for the film industry. In Hollywood, a part of Los Angeles, there are famous film studios. A lot of film stars and well-known people live in Hollywood.

Nearby Los Angeles, in Anaheim, is Disneyland – a funpark, created by Walt Disney. There you can have fun, go along by train, visit adventure land, meet Mickey Mouse, go into space ... It's fascinating to enter a different world – with attractions and fun.

Los Angeles is also famous for its beaches. Santa Monica beach and Venice beach are well-known. There is a wide variety of people. Walking along the street you can find hundreds of inline-skaters, jugglers, clowns and musicians.

Beside watching people you can also go swimming, lie in the sun or ride your surf board. There are fantastic waves and so you can practise surfing.

Because of the sun, the fun you can have and the possibilities of getting a job, California has always been a symbol of sunny life and freedom. In the past it was the same. When gold was found in California in 1848 a lot of people tried to make their fortune in the west. So they moved from east to west by wagon. In the 20th century Route 66 was used to move from east to west, from Chicago to L.A., from Illinois to California, where it ends.

■ Read the text.

■ Look up any new words in a dictionary and write them down in your exercise book.

■ Collect pictures of California. Help: Ask for travel brochures, look for pictures in magazines ...

■ Create a poster showing the sights of California. Try to show California as a sunny state.

Material: dictionary, exercise book, pictures of California, paper, scissors, glue, felt tip marker

WORDFINDER

▩ Read the text "California – the Golden State" once more.

▩ Underline the following words:

    wind
    sun
    waves
    beach
    inline skater
    juggler
    clown
    musician
    surfing
    Mickey Mouse
    space
    adventure
    gold

▩ Find a partner.

▩ Write the words mentioned above on your partner's back. Use your fingers.

▩ He/she has to guess what word is written.

Material: text: "California – the Golden State", ruler

PREPOSITIONS

In the text "California – the Golden State" there are prepositions that describe
a direction – *(to go) by*
a place   – *in*
a time   – *in (the past)*

▨ Underline the prepositions of direction, place and time in the text with three different colours.

▨ Compare your solution with the answer key.

▨ Translate the following sentences.

▨ Compare your sentences with the answer key.

Material: text: "California – the Golden State", ruler

Die Touristen *gehen* den Venice Beach *entlang* und sehen die Schaufenster *an*.

Am Abend *sind vor* den Geschäften viele Musiker.

Die Inline-Skater *zeigen auf* dem Boulevard ihre Kunststücke.

Die Leute *liegen am* Strand *in* der Sonne.

CALIFORNIA DREAMING

California – the Golden State – is and was always a dream land.

■ Put the sentences of the song "California Dreaming" in front of you.

■ Listen to the song.

■ Read the sentences and try to put them in the correct order.

■ Draw a picture showing the contents of the song. Use water colours or a pencil.

Material: cassette recorder or CD-player, recording and text: "California Dreaming"

California Dreaming
(by "The Mamas and the Papas")

All the leaves are brown
And the sky is grey
I've been for a walk
On a winter's day.
I'd be safe and warm
If I was in L.A.
California Dreaming
On such a winter's day.
Stopped into a church
I passed along the way
Well, I get down on my knees,
And I pretend to pray.
You know the preacher likes the cold,
He knows I'm going to stay.
California Dreaming
On such a winter's day.
All the leaves are brown,
And the sky is grey.
I've been for a walk
On a winter's day.
If I didn't tell her,
I could leave today.
California Dreaming
On such a winter's day ...

ANSWER KEY – USA – ROUTE 66

A2

Give a definition of the following words.
Examples:

road: It's a piece of ground which is built between two places so that people can drive or ride from one place to the other.

adventure: It's an event that you become involved in. It can be unusual, exciting or dangerous.

freedom: You are allowed to do and say what you want.

sundown: Another word for sunset. The sun moves down the horizon, it's getting dark.

wind: Air moving across the surface of the earth.

Chevy: Short for: Chevrolet (a car's brand name).

desert: It's a piece of land with very little or even no water.

go west: Moving west.

A3

Fill in the missing words (past tense!).
were, had, had, started, called, opened, caused, dreamt, went, reached, died, made, enjoyed, wanted, went, was, ordered, revived

A4

Try to make a conversation.
I'd like to rent a car.
I'd like a Chevy, please.
I'd like to rent it for four weeks.
I will return the car in Los Angeles.
How much is it?
What is the car insurance for these four weeks?
Are there special rules in the states I will pass through?
Can I pay by credit card?

B1

Try to find a title for each part.
Examples:
The third biggest city of the USA – Chicago
The Chicago School of Architecture and the skyscrapers
Alphonse Capone – a leader of a gang
Gangs made contracts
Al Capone was brought to Alcatraz

B3

Compare the things and persons.
The Empire State Building is higher than the Sears Tower. – The Sears Tower is smaller than the Empire State Building.
Al Capone was more dangerous than Billy the Kid. – Al Capone is more famous than Billy the Kid.
The Chicago Bulls are better than the Yankees. – The Chicago Bulls are more interesting than the Yankees.
The city of Chicago is bigger than St. Louis. – St. Louis is smaller than the city of Chicago.
Frank Lloyd Wright is as famous as Friedensreich Hundertwasser. – Frank Lloyd Wright is more important than Friedensreich Hundertwasser.
Alcatraz is as safe as the Tower of London. – The Tower of London is more famous than Alcatraz.

C3

Fill the right forms into the worksheet.
to go, to go along, driving, to get, to get, to get, looking for, getting

C4

Fill in the missing sentences into the worksheet.
May I have the menu, please? – Yes, please, with milk and sugar! – Yes, please! – I'd like …

D2

Which word doesn't belong to the others? Mark the wrong word in each line.
chicken, money, potatoes, dry, slow, station, river, road, river, January

Find the generic term.
seasons, grain, cattle, mail, drinks, buildings, people, elements

D3

Fill in the right tenses.
am sitting, is, arrived, was, could, told, decided, had waited, had happened, went, heard, ran, was, am relaxing, is, am, am drinking, will go, will be, will take

E2

Connect the words on the left with a word on the right.
Osage – reservation, Cherokee – Indians, Trail – of Tears, peaceful – Cherokee, white – settlers, wagon – train, move – west, hard – journey, government – soldiers

Try to make sentences with these connected words.
Examples:
The Osage reservation is in Oklahoma.
The Cherokee Indians live on a reservation now.
The Trail of Tears was a hard and long journey west.
The peaceful Cherokee lived together with white people.
White settlers wanted to have the Cherokee land because gold was discovered.
12 000 Cherokee moved west in a long wagon train.
It was cold, the Cherokee were hungry or sick – so it was a hard journey.
The Cherokee didn't want to leave, so government soldiers were sent.

E3

Try to find the questions.
1. Did the Cherokee and the white settlers live in peace? 2. Where do the Cherokee live now? 3. Why did they have to leave? 4. How many Cherokee went into the mountains? 5. How far did they have to travel? 6. Why did many of them die? 7. Where did the Cherokee start a new life? 8. Why did they call their journey west the "Trail of Tears"?

E4

Try to read the Indian writing.
high noon, wise man (Indian), to look for, buffalo, to see, trails of a horse, white man with a gun, wise man, to speak, white man with a gun, sun rise, white man with a gun, an Indian camp, wise man, welcome, to speak, friendship, peace

ANSWER KEY – ROUTE 66

Write down the text in complete sentences.
It was high noon. A wise Indian looked for buffalos.
He saw trails of a horse. There was a white man with
a gun. He spoke to the white man with the gun.
At sundown the white man with the gun got to the
Indian camp. The Indians welcomed him. They spoke
together and became friends. So the white man and
the Indians lived in peace.

F1

Fill in the missing words.
largest state, Oil drills, farmland, cowboys, cattle, hard,
ten, fourteen, ten, twelve, railway station, money, bath,
clothes, ranches, ride, horses, rodeos, best cowboy

F2

Try to find the words.
1. cattle, 2. carriage, 3. funnel, 4. locomotive, engine,
5. wagon, 6. whip, 7. cowboy, 8. saloon

F3

Imagine you are a cowboy. What would you do?
Examples:

If I met an Indian …	I would make friends with him.
If I lost cattle …	I would look for them.
If I were robbed …	I would ask for help.
If I were thirsty …	I would drink water.
If I arrived at a railway station…	I would enjoy lying in a bed.
If I had to sleep on the prairie …	I would look for coyotes.
If I got money …	I would buy a farm.
If I had to cross a wild river …	I would ask for help.
If I saw a coyote at night …	I would light a fire.

G3

Fill in the missing nations or nationalities.
the USA, the Americans – Spain, a Spaniard – Germany,
the Germans – a Canadian, the Canadians – Portugal,
a Portuguese – Great Britain, a Briton – a Chinese,
the Chinese – Asia, the Asians – a Puerto Rican, the
Puerto Ricans – Italy, an Italian

G4

Try to write the story.
Example:
Cowboys who met in the saloon of Hadleyville talked
about Frank Miller, a revolver man, who would arrive
in Hadleyville. All the people were afraid.
At the same time Frank Miller sat in the train to
Hadleyville. He looked dangerous.
At high noon Frank Miller arrived in Hadleyville.
All the people of Hadleyville hid in their houses.
Marshall Kane waited for the revolver man in town.
Frank Miller and Marshall Kane met in the street.
Both men were all alone, without any help.
Marshall Kane shot Frank Miller.

H1

Answer the questions and you will get the contents
of the text in short.
The view of the canyon is fantastic.
But it's *difficult to walk down to the bottom* because
it is one mile deep.
You can *start your tour at the tourist center at the
Grand Canyon*.
You have to take *a lot of water with you* because *it is
hot*.
It takes *four hours down to the bottom, but eight
hours back up*.
The problem is *that you walk downhill when you are
fit but uphill when you are tired*.
There is one important *rule: Never leave a hiker alone
in the canyon*.
Rangers often have to help tourists to get back.

H2

Try to find as many words as possible connected with
sports.
football, canoeing, wandering, skiing, swimming,
parachute-jumping, sailing, surfing, weight-lifting,
rowing, handball

H3

Write down park rules.
You must wear hiking shoes. – You must take water
with you. – You mustn't go alone. – You mustn't walk
down and up in one day. – You must/may start early
in the morning. – You mustn't wear sandals. – You
mustn't leave the trail. – You must be prepared. –
You mustn't leave a hiker in the canyon. – You must
get a ranger sometimes. – You may take photos.

H4

Write down a cell-phone-call with a ranger.
We are in the canyon und can't walk anymore!
No, my friend is with me!
We started early in the morning and went down.
Later we went back again.
We are one hour before Cedar Ridge
No, we have drunken all the water.
Okay, thank you! Bye!

I3

Fill in the prepositions.
direction: (to go) by, (to get) into, (to walk) along,
(to move) from, (to move) to
place: in, near by
time: in (the past)

Translate the following sentences.
The tourists walk along Venice Beach and look
at the shop windows.
In the evening there are a lot of musicians in front
of the shops.
Inline skaters show their tricks on the boulevards.
People lie on the beach in the sun.